FIRE PEARLS

SHORT MASTERPIECES

OF THE

HUMAN HEART

EDITED BY M. KEI

TANKA, KYOKA, CINQUAINS, AND MORE

2006
M. KEI, PUBLISHER
PERRYVILLE, MARYLAND

Copyright 2006 by M. Kei. All poems copyright by their respective authors.

Cover image copyright by Michal Milos, used in accordance with the Creative Commons Attribution-ShareAlike 2.0 license.

All rights reserved. No part of this book may be reproduced in any form or by any means, except by a reviewer or scholar who may quote brief passages in a review or article.

No part of this book may be reproduced in any form without the permission of the copyright holder.

Printed in the United States of America

5 4 3 2 1

Published by M. Kei, P. O. Box 1118, Elkton, MD 21922-1118, www.firepearls.com, through Lulu Enterprises, Inc., 3131 RDU Center, Suite 210, Morrisville, NC 27560, www.lulu.com.

ISBN: 978-1-4303-0999-4

to
Denis M. Garrison
and Sanford Goldstein
with deepest appreciation

PREFACE

The book you hold in your hands is an unusual one and bound to become a collector's item. It showcases short poems of five lines each: tanka, kyoka, cinquains, free verse, and more. Most of these forms are not very well known in English, so it is worth a moment to explain them.

The 'tanka' originated in Japan more than 1300 years ago and is still going strong today. A short lyric poem that treats any subject, the human heart has long been a favorite subject—so much so that some Westerners think tanka is solely love poetry. This book will not disabuse them of that notion, but we hasten to point out tanka also embraces nature, philosophy, humor, and just about anything else.

This was not always the case. During the ancient period tanka barred anything violent or vulgar. Naturally, human nature being what it is, poets composed a number of bawdy and humorous verses anyhow. These comic verses were called 'kyoka' (crazy poems). The earliest collection of such work dates to the 13th century.

In the early 20th century, the West encountered Japanese poetry and attempted to meld the tanka aesthetic with Western poetic traditions; the result was the 'cinquain.' The cinquain has enjoyed a minor but growing popularity ever since.

The original Japanese tanka was composed of five lines with a syllable pattern of 5-7-5-7-7, but most poets writing tanka in English do not bother counting syllables. Instead, they seek the most meaning with the fewest possible words. You will find both kinds of poems in this book, and all of them powerfully evoke the passions of the human heart.

This book is divided into five seasons, reflecting the importance of nature and nature imagery in tanka poetry. Spring, Summer, Autumn, and Winter need no explanation, but because the human heart often refuses to live and love in an orderly fashion, a Fifth Season was added to present poems that likewise refuse neat categorization.

Hopefully you, dear reader, will enjoy this book so much that you will seek out more tanka, kyoka, and cinquains: a recommended reading list is in the back of the book. If you are tempted to try writing your own verses, you will also find a list of resources.

A book of this nature is a major undertaking, so I must thank Michael McClintock and Denis M. Garrison. They were instrumental in designing the project and in inviting poets to participate. Thanks are due to Denis especially for his kind assistance with the cover and technical matters. My warmest appreciation goes to Sanford Goldstein for his unfailing enthusiasm and support. Additional thanks go to Michele Kraus, my good friend and proofreader, and to my reader, Amora Johnson, for giving me a Gen Y perspective on an ancient poetic form.

~K~

M. Kei
Perryville, MD
20 August 2006

CONTENTS

✷

PREFACE V

SPRING 11

SUMMER 39

AUTUMN 67

WINTER 95

FIFTH SEASON 123

APPENDICES 153

SPRING

between sun and shade
a butterfly pauses
like none I've seen—
who ever falls in love
with someone they know?

Michael McClintock
United States

sidewalk café
my lunch date tossing bread
to fox sparrows . . .
does he not know I would eat
the crumbs right out of his hand?

an'ya
United States

This morning
surprised to find my back door
unlocked
after last night you slipped again
into my dreams

Angela Leuck
Canada

were
I a Genji
sportsman,
the ride over for the night's mystery
might have been long and sweet

Sanford Goldstein
Japan

SPRING

water in the well
with my palm I skim the pail
to catch stars one by one —
when in the night you visit
I scatter them before you

Vasile Smarandescu
Bucuresti, Romania

for the scent
of her long brown hair,
I lean closer
and point at
any old star

Chad Lee Robinson
United States

whispering
in her ear again —
is it love
or simply because her beautiful ear
resembles a question mark?

André Surridge
New Zealand

FIRE PEARLS

> her laughter
> trails out the window —
> a bevy
> of blue butterflies over
> the moon-washed city
>
> *Larry Kimmel*
> *United States*

> holding hands
> in the gallery —
> one by one
> I see your face
> on the walls
>
> *J. Andrew Lockhart*
> *United States*

> st. patrick's day —
> she notices the green
> after the pinch,
> her kiss heals the wound
> but not the blush
>
> *Dustin Neal*
> *Texas, United States*

SPRING

does your day
pass slowly, like it
does for me? —
remembering the taste
of tobacco on your lips

An Xiao
New York, United States

Racing home
before the storm
I find your letter
in my mailbox &
the first few drops of rain

Angela Leuck
Canada

when you opened
my letter
were you surprised
my heart
fell out?

Michael McClintock
United States

FIRE PEARLS

the boat comes to rest
after twelve days of ocean,
he, bewhiskered and
sunburned, with triumphant smile . . .
I rush to his embrace

Abigail Greene
United States

like a young girl
in love with the deep spring nights
I have returned
tell me what you want tonight
and I will make it yours

Marjorie A. Buettner
United States

your smile
unlocks my heart
wound tight
now I am a bird set free
singing long into the night

André Surridge
New Zealand

SPRING

Like Gauguin's
violet lover
palm open
I offer this
raw heart.

Pamela Miller Ness
United States

well-loved and wise,
the careful goddess
who in the morning
brushes all sorrow
from her hair

Michael McClintock
United States

my hands
around the morning cup
of green tea
this man who loves me
near enough to feel my breath

Patricia Prime
New Zealand

FIRE PEARLS

    the sky
    curves around the earth
    meeting itself
    seamlessly your tenderness
    encircles each of my days

    Janice Bostok
    Australia

    full of spring bulbs
    and parked on its shadow —
    the wheelbarrow . . .
    my pregnant wife at rest
    in mid-afternoon shade

    an'ya
    United States

    in the breeze
    a flag lifts and falls
    with slow abandon
    bringing thoughts of you
    and the night ahead

    Thelma Mariano
    Canada

SPRING

her skirt brightens
in the sunlight at the door—
quick! quick!
    her scissor shadow
        cuts me through

Larry Kimmel
United States

mesmerized
as you come to me
lover legs
kicking the world
off the bedroom stairs

Jack Prewitt
Australia

brazen and
beautiful I grasp him
by the tail of his dreams
feeling alive for the
first time in life

Orestes
United States

FIRE PEARLS

    she reached
    from behind me
    on a motorcycle
    no place then
    was impossible

    Dave Bacharach
    United States

    like the climbing rose
    let my arms encircle
    your brown torso
    whisper in my ear
    to make me bloom

    John Daleiden
    United States

    In my mother's garden
    one exotic black tulip
    bloomed wild
    tonight my fingers stroke
    my lover's ebony skin

    Angela Leuck
    Canada

SPRING

electrify me—
spin your youth in a charm,
awaken runes
dormant with age and distance,
ripen once more this old tree

John Daleiden
United States

Freya's heart shape
is not blood pulsating
in a male's chest
but the secret throbbing
of our female desire

Janice Bostok
Australia

he is writing
a poem with his tongue
on my neck
in a foreign language
only we can understand

Patricia Prime
New Zealand

a thousand tanka
yearn for you, I wish
no more paper
only the living tree
and under it, you

Bernard Gadd
New Zealand

almost full, the moon
draped with a thin cloud
no privacy from the poets
who try to write this love
we share under the willow

Dustin Neal
Texas, United States

the way you are sleeping,
the smile on your lips —
if this were my darkest hour
I would have no need
to wake you now

John Barlow
United Kingdom

SPRING

morning sun
warming our sheets . . .
for a moment
as you slide your body down,
your nipple in my navel

Michael Dylan Welch
Sammamish, Washington, United States

stark from the shower
to answer the phone,
she dons a robe
of the finest distance —
the girl with spring desire

Larry Kimmel
United States

how can i bathe myself
so soon after you've left? —
the scent of you
upon my lips, my throat
my breasts, my thighs

An Xiao
New York, United States

FIRE PEARLS

> she runs topless
> out to her car
> for lipstick
> the next morning Joe
> my neighbor smiles
>
> *Dave Bacharach*
> *United States*

> her camisole
> left on the bed
> with clean sheets —
> dream and reality
> meet for one moment
>
> *J. Andrew Lockhart*
> *United States*

> in the morning
> we rise and part for work —
> each day is full
> the chocolate morsel at lunch
> swells my thoughts of your delights
>
> *John Daleiden*
> *United States*

SPRING

each year, for you
a box of birthday chocolates . . .
what's yours is mine?
how neatly I slice in two
the pieces for you to share

Janet Lynn Davis
Houston, Texas, United States

we run up the street
under each lamp kiss
even as windows open . . .
memory watches
your unchanging smile

Bernard Gadd
New Zealand

a half-moon
in afternoon blue sky
and the two of us
probably three quarters
into our relationship

John Barlow
United Kingdom

his girlfriend Heather
moody as the Yorkshire moors
from sunlight and smiles
to dark unrelenting rain
in the flicker of an eye

André Surridge
New Zealand

She is no moon yet
she drifts like the moon, takes care
of him from the sky —
meets him for a short, waxing
leaves him for a long, waning

R. K. Singh
India

following you home
to a backwoods cabin
I glimpse a firefly
in the shadows of your heart
that no one will ever catch

Darrell Lindsey
United States

because I love you,
your detachment can be
devastating and
I have learned that love does not
entitle ownership

Abigail Greene
United States

nevermind
the ten thousand footsteps
rushing around me—
the simple thought of you
shall leave me lonely

An Xiao
New York, United States

I am awake tonight
not because of a bright moon
or lovesickness,
but mere insomnia—and you,
you would not care the reason

Michael Dylan Welch
Sammamish, Washington, United States

FIRE PEARLS

       I'd sleep
       if sleep were safe,
       but I fear
       the ruin
       of my dreams.

       M. Kei
       Chesapeake Bay, United States

       at dawn potted plants
       bend towards each other
       i would lean
       into your light if you
       would make the offer

       Janice Bostok
       Australia

       she believes
       I don't really love her—
       red garden rose
       about to bloom
       please forgive me

       George Swede
       Canada

SPRING

my wife has learned
that asphalt is a mix
of sand and oil—
I wonder what more
may she learn of me

Tom Clausen
United States

unable to see
the darkside of the moon
i wish to consult
a clairvoyant who can
and will tell me about us

Janice Bostok
Australia

Valentine's day:
the morning paper has
three articles on love
which we read with thoughts
unexpressed

George Swede
Canada

FIRE PEARLS

> fist poised to knock
> I hear two voices within—
> the irises nod
> and whisper as I retrace my steps
> along her flagstone walk
>
> *Larry Kimmel*
> *United States*

> moonlight filters
> through my room stirring feelings
> I can't explain
> this wave of longing for you
> as I lie so close to him
>
> *Thelma Mariano*
> *Canada*

> as I lie still,
> you interrupt my
> late night thoughts
> ignoring what was
> while hanging on what wasn't
>
> *J. Andrew Lockhart*
> *United States*

SPRING

the green-eyed monster,
my inadequacies
bloomed large in my soul,
you must have found me Hell
to put up with back then

Abigail Greene
United States

saying goodbye
on the table between us
an amaryllis bud
just beginning
    to open

Margaret Chula
United States

you can leave
me if you wish —
i doubt i'd
want me either,
a woman deformed

An Xiao
New York, United States

along the river
where trees are glad with leaflets,
she had to tell me—
later, pitched across the hotel bed,
I wept

Larry Kimmel
United States

the limit of enough
seems to expand another
ninety-degrees:
I want a red kite-flight to tug
this fragile white string a while longer

Sanford Goldstein
Japan

where will you go
when breakfast is over
and dreams stare
up at me from a
chalice of shadow?

Robert D. Wilson
United States/Philippines

SPRING

Ruined pears,
bruised brown, fall to the grass
and spill their juice.
We should lie together, warm
under the death-watch of the sky.

Penny Harter
New Jersey, United States

again
with the wrong key
I fumble
only for a moment
this time

Brenda Humphrey-McMahen
Florida, United States

after supporting
their divorce plans
I write them a Valentine;
suggest they reconsider
it all again

Tom Clausen
United States

FIRE PEARLS

    The Pacific
    and the Indian Ocean
    and the Atlantic too
    drown his words
    "Marriage won't make you happy."

    M. Kei
    Chesapeake Bay, United States

    crows perch
    on the court-house fence
    wings flit
    as does my heart
    when the judge's gavel bangs

    Janice Bostok
    Australia

    his reflection
    in a window of stars
    hesitant
    to ask her
    to call his father

    Brenda Humphrey-McMahen
    Florida, United States

pressed
against the windowpane
our daughter's palm print
as if
it could coax him to return

Linda Jeannette Ward
United States

my stolen
Valentine pendant,
at its center
a golden, mythical bird
wings no longer mine

Janet Lynn Davis
Houston, Texas, United States

the ancient masters
could find words in each blossom
but in fallen times
there are a hundred petals
for every word I know

Jim Kacian
United States

FIRE PEARLS

> so lonely
> again this night . . .
> the moonlight
> spills over the levee
> toward your street
>
> *Michael Dylan Welch*
> *Sammamish, Washington, United States*

> the dawn's gray effusion grieves
> for lack of color,
> lack of warmth—
>   all I know of love
>   wouldn't fill a sonnet
>
> *Larry Kimmel*
> *United States*

> Spot my old flame
> buying Gitanes
> & the New York Times—
> not to trouble his heart
> I slip from the shop
>
> *Marianne Bluger*
> *Canada*

SPRING

my worn out sandals
the cobbler finds it
difficult to mend
and i find it hard
to discard

Kala Ramesh
India

thirty years later
the pale blue petals
pressed in my journal
what was that flower — and
who was that man?

Margaret Chula
United States

when there are
so many stars
in the sky,
why can't I find
one for me?

M. Kei
Chesapeake Bay, United States

SUMMER

june
and the clouds paint
jackson pollock numbers
in monochrome
just for us

John Barlow
United Kingdom

FIRE PEARLS

> In tonight's sky
> silent lightning—
> when I see you
> there are no words
> to express this longing
>
> *Angela Leuck*
> *Canada*

> the thrill
> of first rains
> in my hands
> your hands
> first time I held
>
> *Kala Ramesh*
> *India*

> high humidity
> a swollen red sun hangs
> heavily in the air
> I slip on the silk dress
> and it feels like rain on skin
>
> *Marjorie A. Buettner*
> *United States*

SUMMER

skinny dipping
in the Gihon River
on the summer solstice
    jangle of my bracelets
    my quickening heart

Margaret Chula
United States

in this tiny cove
I'm a skin's width
from the water and sun,
the cliffs' reflections,
and the light of you

Bernard Gadd
New Zealand

salt on my tongue
pulled into his body's curve
I dream of conches
that curl into my palm
and whisper of the sea

Beverley George
Pearl Beach, Australia

FIRE PEARLS

creek a vivid green
mangrove leaves dull
tussocks dusty
but your back gleams
sea salt brown and white

Bernard Gadd
New Zealand

black man
cretan pearl — too
priceless yet common.
he's beautifully wrapped
within my breath.

Orestes
United States

rain-furled hibiscus —
in the slow refolding
of our secret places
we draw even closer
than at passion's zenith

Beverley George
Pearl Beach, Australia

SUMMER

biting
into the peach
it seemed
it did
kiss me

Michael McClintock
United States

her breast fits
like a fruit in the curve
of the small guitar—
and I would be her Picasso
some Spanish afternoon

Larry Kimmel
United States

your voice, an echo,
chasing dreams that keep
me up at night,
when mango moon lifts
up her blouse . . . and smiles

Robert D. Wilson
United States/Philippines

grasp him by the ears
listen to the rust-colored
song sailing thru his
apricot veins . . . he must be
the one to capture my soul.

Orestes
United States

when Lilith rises
playing her tenor sax
the world goes green
stone statues dance and
butcher-blocks burst into bloom

Denis M. Garrison
United States

how on earth
did you pick me
out of the crowd . . .
bright stars
and drunken sailors

Andrew Riutta
United States

SUMMER

The time
you asked me
to marry you
how haughtily I marched away
when we were eight

Angela Leuck
Canada

Queen Anne's Lace and
Black-Eyed Susans
by the thousands along the road
and to think
you married me

Tom Clausen
United States

big decision now,
she lingers in the bathroom,
to wear, or not,
her rhinestone earrings on
this, their wedding night

Abigail Greene
United States

45

spent, side by side—
we watch spilled stars brighten
in velvet blackness
can you ever know the depth
of my love for you?

John Daleiden
United States

Sultry dawn—
waking to the scent
of aftershave,
five fresh sunflowers
on the kitchen table.

Pamela Miller Ness
United States

moored in quiet,
i stare past the stars
into a morning
borrowed
from your smile

Robert D. Wilson
United States/Philippines

SUMMER

frayed brown grasses
dormant in the June sun—
the call of a crow
in the stillness at sunrise
I kiss your bare shoulder

John Daleiden
United States

Sampling
this year's strawberries
from the market
how much better they tasted—
the ones we picked by moonlight

Angela Leuck
Canada

Tempted to try it
he loves me,
he loves me not
    my hand reaches out
    towards the white daisy

Margaret Chula
United States

in the mid-day heat—
undesirable plants grow
with great passion
I cultivate our tidy
garden, clipping spent blooms

John Daleiden
United States

passion,
you call it? others
chide me—
whirling those pages of anguish
round a low Japanese table

Sanford Goldstein
Japan

what I said
what she said
on the porch
sweeping dust
back and forth

Chad Lee Robinson
United States

SUMMER

this summer day
I've swum the English Channel,
vacuumed, scrubbed, dusted;
then run the dishwasher thrice—
and all before it's bedtime

an'ya
United States

wondering
why I leave you
alone
you watch
another sunset

Brenda Humphrey-McMahen
Florida, United States

Into the garbage
the remains of the day—
if only these could include
some of the words
we said

George Swede
Canada

FIRE PEARLS

    the gorgeous
    generosity
    of my kid
    tiptoeing along the edge
    of tonight's roughness

    Sanford Goldstein
    Japan

    tired of arguing
    we cool off
    on the porch
    with what's left
    of the stars

    Chad Lee Robinson
    United States

    this morning, still
    the bitterness
    of our argument
        I pluck slugs
        off the peony buds

    Margaret Chula
    United States

SUMMER

fragments of lotus
after the storm . . .
unlike a woman who
must endure
the long rainy season

Pamela A. Babusci
Rochester, New York, United States

In the living room
my make-up roses bent
towards the nearest window
red petals open wide
to the new day

George Swede
Canada

What he
whispered to me
in the train car, snatched out
by the mountain tunnel . . . Was it
". . . love you"?

Zhanna P. Rader
United States/Russia

51

the storm over
a sharp new moon
pierces black sky
the scent of your breath
clings to my pillow

Janice Bostok
Australia

on the beach that night
with a thousand stars
I didn't miss you
until I finally returned
and found you asleep

Thelma Mariano
Canada

another ball game
and she wonders why
I'm so taken by the win and lose
as if our lives were
nothing like that

Tom Clausen
United States

SUMMER

Hanging out the wash
I try to comprehend
this changeable sky
such a simple thing compared
to reading your heart

Angela Leuck
Canada

the field
and the poet
s i l e n c e
where you once told me
you loved my poems

Dustin Neal
Texas, United States

next door
the lovemaking
subsides
stars fall
from other worlds

Michael McClintock
United States

the stranger
I made love to
in last night's dream
I meet at the farmers' market
—his toddler in hand

Margaret Chula
United States

rip-tide
slowly I return
an occupied shell
to the surging sea
between us

Beverley George
Pearl Beach, Australia

the night before
she's scheduled to leave
the philippines,
i couldn't sleep . . .
her voice treading water

Robert D. Wilson
United States/Philippines

SUMMER

must I too
live all by myself like
the hermit crab?
in a pink-walled castle
with no room for a queen

a*n'ya*
United States

the pale blue dress will
insure me some man's embrace
tonight when jazz beats
melt inside cigarette smoke,
leaving no room for regrets.

Orestes
United States

in a cocktail
dress covered with sequins,
the moon saunters
past me into
another man's bed

Robert D. Wilson
United States/Philippines

FIRE PEARLS

Moment by moment
pendulum ticks the tempo
of a melody;
we are unwilling dancers
in an anonymous whirl

Magdalena Dale
Romania

I show him how much
I love and desire him—
then he goes home to her.
I want to hammer nails
through both of them.

M. Kei
Chesapeake Bay, United States

buried
in low clouds
the steeple
reminds me of the wine
that clouded our judgment

Dustin Neal
Texs, United States

SUMMER

ten centuries ago
in courtly Japan you'd
have sent me a poem—
after our night together
what can i hope to receive?

An Xiao
New York, United States

a volley of hailstones
bouncing off
drought-cracked fields—
another new romance
that can't replace you

Linda Jeannette Ward
United States

traveling a country
far too barren to love,
we changed for good
in that bleak motel,
having only each other

Michael McClintock
United States

FIRE PEARLS

"I couldn't help myself"
that's what she said,
and all this long day's journey into night
   imagination
     an intolerable jingle

Larry Kimmel
United States

The comb she dropped
broke when I stepped on it
by accident,
but I enjoyed
the sound of spite.

M. Kei
Chesapeake Bay, United States

second time around —
you hold me tighter now
even in sleep
lest I visit the place
where old wounds lie

Thelma Mariano
Canada

SUMMER

will the sweet taste of
small melons under a
full moon, carry me
across this dark river of
second hand dreams?

Robert D. Wilson
United States/Philippines

Too late
for us to dream
the dreams of happiness—
our road has forked, meandering,
and yet.

Zhanna P. Rader
United States/Russia

from my hill
I watch you pick up and re-read
the letter I left you
in that secret place we promised
never again to visit

Michael McClintock
United States

FIRE PEARLS

Going out to view
the full moon, but finding it
hidden in fog
the old longing draws me
ever closer to your door

Angela Leuck
Canada

this time, she tells me,
she's telling the truth—
between us
I watch the struggles of a wasp
drowning in peach juice

Larry Kimmel
United States

rattlesnake love—
you gave me warning
but I, entranced
by your desert heart,
wouldn't heed it

M. Kei
Chesapeake Bay, United States

SUMMER

taking a walk
so she can be alone
with her lover
he ponders imperfection
and fingers his ring

Dave Bacharach
United States

truth lies
shrouded in maya
and beneath the veil
once lifted
truth lies

Kala Ramesh
India

water lilies
floating
effortlessly . . .
how difficult it was to
leave my unfaithful lover

Pamela A. Babusci
Rochester, New York, United States

cold wind
divorce papers served
the bottom falling out
of a distant cloud
rainshower

susan delphine delaney
United States

I sign
on the blank line
my name
the only thing
you left me

Brenda Humphrey-McMahen
Florida, United States

the cuckoo clock strikes
I smile at the soft dawn light
until my eyes rest
on your bare dressing table,
on all the empty hangers

Denis M. Garrison
United States

SUMMER

dusk . . .
she walks through a field
of photographs
where she first
kissed my smile

Dustin Neal
Texas, United States

sometimes i think
i can still see you waiting
for me —
the bar where we first met
on our East Village date

An Xiao
New York, United States

after many years
the sound of your voice
on the telephone
rain is dripping
from just-budded trees

Margaret Chula
United States

our old table
and the place hasn't changed
a bit—
if it wasn't for the glint
of her diamond . . .

Larry Kimmel
United States

What he has—
I'm not just
green with envy,
my heart
is passionate jade.

M. Kei
Chesapeake Bay, United States

in the parking lot
a black bird
pecks at pecans
along with the black man
who holds a wedding invitation

Dustin Neal
Texas, United States

SUMMER

at his request
our son between us
we pose
without the stepparents
a stranger and his mother

Brenda Humphrey-McMahen
Florida, United States

ten years later . . .
both married with one child
we all pass on a path
and smile politely
without a word

Tom Clausen
United States

AUTUMN

every road
that ends in fallen leaves
leads to you . . .
the moon in your cauldron
the earth on your knees

Andrew Riutta
United States

cricket song at dusk
the charcoal smell of salmon
fills my senses
beside you in firelight
all my longings vanish

John Daleiden
United States

cool autumn's wind
reaches the open window
and enters slowly
then I am in your embrace
warmed by your breath in my hair

Marjorie A. Buettner
United States

that small sere leaf
in my hair was a moth
you untangled . . .
a single strand of my hair
between your white teeth

Patricia Prime
New Zealand

AUTUMN

not a breath
of autumn wind
at twilight
now can you hear
my beating heart?

Jim Kacian
United States

When my boys are here
    the autumn nights fly past like
        swallows in the dusk.
Autumn nights are long
    only by repute.

M. Kei
Chesapeake Bay, United States

the circling moon
colors the depth of the night
with a golden light
for the briefest of moments
tasting your lips once again

Marjorie A. Buettner
United States

FIRE PEARLS

> his body glows with
> the inner stem of incense
> smoke speaking to the
> winds . . . skating along the coast
> of the moon . . . with him . . . I'm good.
>
> *Orestes*
> *United States*

> the fluid motion
> of hands on African drums
> a staccato beat
> like the constant rhythm
> that plays out between us
>
> *Thelma Mariano*
> *Canada*

> standing in the wings
> drowning in the burnished sound
> of his baritone;
> his eyes connected with mine,
> soon we duet-melody.
>
> *Orestes*
> *United States*

AUTUMN

When I see you here
My heart is set fluttering
In my eager breast
I hear your seraphic voice
And I am paler than grass.

Claire Elliott
United Kingdom

when I was twenty
I sang like Mozart's
Queen of the Night
    now I hum like a cello
    between the legs of a lover

Margaret Chula
United States

a knock on the door
two am and the pre-morning
kisses lust in him.
black man, turned built black oak,
walks in his system with sweet sin.

Orestes
United States

FIRE PEARLS

Wrestling for dominance,
he's taller, but I'm stronger.
I pin him to the bed
and make him admit
he loves me.

M. Kei
Chesapeake Bay, United States

The piano idle for weeks
yet this moonless night she plays
The Moonlight Sonata . . .
dust specks spiral towards
the overhead light

George Swede
Canada

I took her
against a stone wall
in freezing rain
someone said that she
got married . . . had kids

Dave Bacharach
United States

AUTUMN

Cold fire
of a carat diamond
on her tiny hand
she has accomplished
all she planned

Marianne Bluger
Canada

I harness the horse
to fetch the Great Bear for you
down to the backyard—
the orchestra tunes to A
to intone the Wedding March

Vasile Smarandescu
Bucuresti, Romania

as the cold gurney
shudder-squeaks down the hall
for one more exam
your hand in mine
makes us safe

Denis M. Garrison
United States

FIRE PEARLS

With melting flakes
still spangling his parka
he lies down
by my side on the hospital bed
& I'm home

Marianne Bluger
Canada

downtown—
dirt ice sickles hang
from the minivan
we purchased for our
miscarried child

Dustin Neal
Texas, United States

dear little baby,
you had only just begun,
we named you Martha,
there is a hole without you,
I wonder what you'd be like

Abigail Greene
United States

AUTUMN

a light-filled face
in your curtained room
the bassinet
contains the first-born child
somewhat yellow with jaundice

Patricia Prime
New Zealand

her newborn face
smaller than your open hand;
this daughter
has no idea yet
how safe she is

Janet Lynn Davis
Houston, Texas, United States

my three tanka
on the back seat —
David
Rachel
Lisa

Sanford Goldstein
Japan

FIRE PEARLS

> the professor's son
> gets a B in Math; still, he knows
> about finite sets—
> the little ways his Dad
> will choose to show displeasure
>
> *Linda Morey Papanicolaou*
> *Palo Alto, California, United States*

> tiptoeing
> through the badlands
> my son
> wanting to be bad
> while walking the line
>
> *shanna baldwin moore*
> *United States*

> seeing my children
> with their families
> I realize
> their centre of gravity
> has shifted
>
> *Kala Ramesh*
> *India*

AUTUMN

high clouds . . .
one horse leans in
against another —
before our children
my wife and I were like that

Tom Clausen
United States

so handsome
in his forest-green shirt
my husband
gently asking me
for a few hours alone

Laura Maffei
United States

after a rough day
she props her head in hand
a few inches from my face
and asks intently:
"do you really like me?"

Tom Clausen
United States

FIRE PEARLS

        embarrassed
        our love making not going well
        this morning
        i look away as he tries
        a street kid's skateboard

Janice Bostok
Australia

        there is no more
        spontaneity in our
        lovemaking these years,
        after prostate surgery and
        the onset of Lavitra

Abigail Greene
United States

        you speak of the distance
        between us now
        yet still I remember
        the smallness of your breasts,
        how they delighted me

Michael Dylan Welch
Sammamish, Washington, United States

AUTUMN

The nightgown sleep-strayed
from the still young-looking bum
she didn't let me touch earlier—
my hand becomes one
with a moonbeam

George Swede
Canada

I remember when
some Sundays were spent in bed,
getting to know each
other's bodies, to please,
now, Sundays, we go to church

Abigail Greene
United States

Another day closer
to the end of my life
without lovemaking—
a blue jay is screeching
in the bare maple

George Swede
Canada

FIRE PEARLS

      nun of your
      bedchamber
      I wear
      the habit
      of your flesh

Penny Harter
New Jersey, United States

      they say the moon
      little by little each day
      moves away
      I confess to no one
      what strangers we have become

Marjorie A. Buettner
United States

      Two swans
      in our old pond—
      one black, the other white.
      Why can't we be as happy as
      they are?

Zhanna P. Rader
United States/Russia

AUTUMN

she asks
are you happy
I say yes—
that's close enough
to what I mean

Dave Bacharach
United States

leaving a warm bed
to write the lines that come
before sleep—
I hold my face to the rain
falling from another world

Michael McClintock
United States

in my pocket
words from you—
cranes fly
across the face
of the mountain

Penny Harter
New Jersey, United States

what words would
convince you to stay?
this autumn heart
shedding leaves
like a scarlet maple

Pamela A. Babusci
Rochester, New York, United States

the clouds
are in the river
so clear
this conversation
is over

Brenda Humphrey-McMahen
Florida, United States

One thousand miles
travelling together
in tense silence
he and she contemplate
the next round of duel

R. K. Singh
India

AUTUMN

back road
a question mark of rain
in the middle rut
and in it the stars
and my face

Jim Kacian
United States

it glides towards me
as I sit at the harbor
in our time apart
trying not to think of you —
the sailboat without a sail

Thelma Mariano
Canada

wind's bitter
spray burns
on the pitching launch
I want to hold you still
warm and firm

Bernard Gadd
New Zealand

the sea
so harsh tonight
wave after wave
dragging back
our sleepless silence

John Barlow
United Kingdom

you never showed up
at the train station
   as it empties
   I learn the cell-phone's
   re-dial function

Michael McClintock
United States

in the night-fog
a yellow bruise
where the streetlight was—
any truth is better
than indefinite doubt

Larry Kimmel
United States

AUTUMN

brown stems
catching snow
too late
in the season
for another mistake

Brenda Humphrey-McMahen
Florida, United States

tonight's snow
falls like a shroud
outside my window
how to shake this feeling
that I won't see you again

Thelma Mariano
Canada

I was not lonely
with the snow-capped heron
as my company,
but when my lover returned
the silence was desolate.

M. Kei
Chesapeake Bay, United States

FIRE PEARLS

    when I left
    this morning she said
    I hate you
    all day I consider
    the reds of autumn

    Dave Bacharach
    United States

    late in the season
    I watch the last geese fly south
    alone in the cold
    is how I make up my mind
    to finally tell you goodbye

    Thelma Mariano
    Canada

    before you move out
    I lie in an empty bath
    contemplating life
    without even your back brush
    and splashproof fish radio

    John Barlow
    United Kingdom

AUTUMN

Gazing out
at maples newly bare
after last night's fierce wind
stripped away too
my last hopes of you

Angela Leuck
Canada

snow sifting
between the shoots
of winter wheat
we begin
our trial separation

susan delphine delaney
United States

from the window
I watch as you leave
taking
our son's hand
and his every other weekend

Brenda Humphrey-McMahen
Florida, United States

FIRE PEARLS

home early
on a winter afternoon
house empty
a garden of dead flowers
but the dog on the doorstep

Jack Prewitt
Australia

the telephone is
our only connection
and barrier—
both outside
looking at the moon

J. Andrew Lockhart
United States

you knew i
wouldn't come back;
your eyes a
neon light blinking
too late! too late!

Robert D. Wilson
United States/Philippines

AUTUMN

if only I knew
you were going forever
I would have met
your dark eyes longer
with that last goodbye

André Surridge
New Zealand

this winter
if you feed the birds
don't stop
she said, then left
and never came back

Dave Bacharach
United States

before you my life
was worth whatever wind blew
against chainlink fence . . .
after you, that trash became
bits and pieces of my heart

an'ya
United States

FIRE PEARLS

all night
I walk the dark street
in my duffel coat
pushing the baby's pram—
leaving you is not easy

Patricia Prime
New Zealand

you have gone
last night
every last leaf
fell
from our gingko

susan delphine delaney
United States

You painted over
the lush green walls
of your room
the day after you go
everything touched with frost

Angela Leuck
Canada

AUTUMN

a drizzly day,
with yellow leaves pasted
to wet black pavement—
returning the library books
she left behind

Larry Kimmel
United States

foolish,
having thought love
would keep us warm;
I chop wood in winter
while you sleep late in Rome

Michael McClintock
United States

lights on the river
where the dredges work
through the night
I drink alone, wondering
why you had to leave

Denis M. Garrison
United States

FIRE PEARLS

before snow fell
she ran off to the desert
later I found
a red-tailed hawk
deep inside my freezer

Dave Bacharach
United States

a few leaves left
on the tree
and me here unable to live
with or without
the love I so desperately sought

Tom Clausen
United States

please don't tell me
about your cat's new litter
already the promise
of these open fields
has changed to loneliness

Penny Harter
New Jersey, United States

AUTUMN

White birch
with black-streaked trunk,
How many Russian girls
have hugged you, crying for their long
lost loves?

Zhanna P. Rader
United States/Russia

"Meet me tomorrow"
your love note said—
I tuck it away
in the old school notebook
and pour a large Scotch

Michael McClintock
United States

the way
all of life once focused
in that one area
as if love and passion
were the grail of grails

Sanford Goldstein
Japan

WINTER

A pearl of rain
trembles at the tip
of a holly leaf.
She passes by
and my heart falls.

M. Kei
Chesapeake Bay, United States

FIRE PEARLS

Sleepless tonight
I wonder what it would be like
to lie in his arms
as the January frost
on the window melts

Angela Leuck
Canada

winter sunlight
for a moment sits
on the bench
where we first shared
a moonlit kiss

Dustin Neal
Texas, United States

the tilt
of her head to undo
an earring—
fortresses crumble into
winter moonlight

Larry Kimmel
United States

WINTER

tonight
I'm going to count
the stars—
if you wait up for me
I might bring back a few

Michael McClintock
United States

coming to bed
I watch you sleeping
in the last light
of the candle
you lit for me

John Barlow
United Kingdom

this moonless night
this hush
of falling snow—
   by lamplight
   your five haiku

Larry Kimmel
United States

FIRE PEARLS

deep wilderness
not one sound echoing
through the arc of trees
but my heart, this chambered heart,
is wild for you tonight

Marjorie A. Buettner
United States

Nose so pressed
to peignoir
that the folds go in
and out
with each short breath

Guy Simser
Ottawa, Canada

your body
tight into mine
over the tenements
the pale moon
crosses the sky

John Barlow
United Kingdom

WINTER

our heads so close
I mistake your hair
to be mine—
on the branch a snow owl
gives a lone call

Kala Ramesh
India

deep
sleeping midnight
my lover
arouses
a rising moon

Pamela Miller Ness
United States

dark side of the moon
becoming the universe
except
for curled toes
and a cheshire smile

Michael R. Goode
United States

FIRE PEARLS

lone call
of the screech owl
bridging
midnight to dawn
you, snoring beside me

Margaret Chula
United States

do you remember
the December you were ill?
you napped on the couch
and we made love to welcome
you back to life

Abigail Greene
United States

dawn
and you open
your deep-green eyes—
blackbirds stir
somewhere in the conifers

John Barlow
United Kingdom

WINTER

first light
you pull me
under the fir
to listen to the sound
of snow falling

susan delphine delaney
United States

Awake in bed I
tremble in memory of
your skin against mine,
wishing it was tomorrow
when tonight is not yet done.

M. Kei
Chesapeake Bay, United States

cold winter Monday
out on the commercial road
stop for a latte
warming the bowl in my hand
thinking of you still in bed

André Surridge
New Zealand

FIRE PEARLS

       maybe we'll meet again
       in the fullness of tomorrow's moon
       alone in my room
       I notice how smoothly my jeans
       slide off my hips

       Thelma Mariano
       Canada

       snow
       about to fall . . .
       both of us know
       we have both
       been waiting

       John Barlow
       United Kingdom

       Snowy morning
       a flock of sparrows
       on bare branches
       all these fears of losing you
       I clap my hands and they scatter

       Angela Leuck
       Canada

WINTER

winter wedding
the cheeky message written
in lipstick on our window
hardens in ice and snow
remaining for the next week

Patricia Prime
New Zealand

Malay restaurant
where once or twice I'd dined
with a lover—
savouring the dishes more
with my husband tonight

Amelia Fielden
Australia

salt and pepper
together on our table—
you lift them
and swoosh off the tablecloth,
set them down again, touching

Michael Dylan Welch
Sammamish, Washington, United States

winter afternoon
warmed
by fig jam
handmade
by my godmother

susan delphine delaney
United States

in the company of friends
our marriage takes on
an air of comfort
as we all attend to things
other than ourselves

Tom Clausen
United States

so much effort
into the building
of my rural house
and the excitement
of these Douglas fir walls!

Sanford Goldstein
Japan

WINTER

our ladder propped
against the gutter—
you turn to see
if I am here
steadying it

Michael Dylan Welch
Sammamish, Washington, United States

late
this frenetic evening
my husband
massages me
until I stop talking

Laura Maffei
United States

my hand reaches
towards the warmth
of a long haired cat
curving into itself—
the night comes closer

Janice Bostok
Australia

deep in snow
the wild beach where we found
this black stone
smooth against my cheek
warm from the wood stove

Kirsty Karkow
United States

when I die
mould an amber amulet
with my ash
wear it around your neck
dangling in your brown breasts

John Daleiden
United States

she's died so early
not even fifty yet,
that golden summer ago
when some of us boys saw
daylight between her breasts

Tom Clausen
United States

WINTER

the best shot in his unit,
he always took point;
at home he took aim
at the enemy in his head
and pulled the trigger

M. Kei
Chesapeake Bay, United States

Tamura out into the sea
Mishima with a sword
and others I could name with pills—
tonight
I count these ways of dying

Sanford Goldstein
Japan

my friend died
last night, I'm told
long distance
I go up to fix the fence
where the horse got out

Dave Bacharach
United States

snow lakes
iceboats cutting
across the winter
my young heart
cracking

M. Kei
Chesapeake Bay, United States

First day back
after the funeral
reaching for the phone to call home
as I have each lunchtime
for fifteen years

Larry Neily
Ottawa, Canada

dead moth
at the edge of the drain
winter still
though it was summer
when you took your last breath

Dustin Neal
Texas, United States

WINTER

dreaming of lola
in my empty bedroom—
how can death
be so real tonight
12 time zones away?

An Xiao
New York, United States

I cannot scatter
your ashes
collected in this urn
my heart
in a thousand pieces

Linda Jeannette Ward
United States

she's not here
to see it
but after breaking the stick
I perfectly fit the broken ends
back together again

Tom Clausen
United States

territorial call
of the kookaburra
announces
this land belongs to you
even in death

Janice Bostok
Australia

I remember now
how the color of the sky
kept me there
the night
of your passing

Brenda Humphrey-McMahen
Florida, United States

when alive I wanted
others to praise our kids
now — he's no more
all I want to hear
are his words

Kala Ramesh
India

WINTER

knees dusted with snow
the mangroves are still
waiting for you
house in the clearing . . .
the bed we once shared

Denis M. Garrison
United States

She senses all things
changing as she passes through
the city again:
should I leave the old house or
lie in the grave before death

R. K. Singh
India

our earthly relationship
so physical and warm
from the other side
you visit me
but we cannot touch

Janice Bostok
Australia

FIRE PEARLS

no net
on earth—no words
might catch her;
I write with ink
made of ashes

Michael McClintock
United States

hard winter
huddling around an open fire
villagers talk and laugh—
within the warmth of my house
I face this utter loneliness

Kala Ramesh
India

mourners assemble
after Joe's funeral—
they come
to pick widow Green's apples
and press out the amber juice

John Daleiden
United States

WINTER

to love
to be loved
either or both
this last midnight
of the year

Sanford Goldstein
Japan

when you were gone
the house was soundless
your memory contracted
into a core so dense
no other love could come close

Patricia Prime
New Zealand

none of my rings
fit this winter
leaving them off
i become
a widow at last

Janice Bostok
Australia

FIRE PEARLS

rest
dear wife
from no-thought
from riddles of the universe
from the master's command

Sanford Goldstein
Japan

years on my own
I still stare after
a white-haired couple
the way his body
shields her from the wind

Thelma Mariano
Canada

frozen pond
how it groans and moans . . .
as it cracks
I understand the pain
of opening to one's depths

Kirsty Karkow
United States

WINTER

in cold hands . . .
the remnant
of a hymnal
her husband passed down
from his first wife

Dustin Neal
Texas, United States

Tidy and comfortable,
this new woman of mine,
pretty, too, and passionate;
but she knows why
my eyes turn to the moon

M. Kei
Chesapeake Bay, United States

when i think i know
everything about love
i fall in love again
for the
first time

Pamela A. Babusci
Rochester, New York, United States

FIRE PEARLS

> my heart
> has been in hibernation
> since you went away —
> call it love or what you will
> snow melts when I think of you
>
> *André Surridge*
> *New Zealand*

> there's always phone,
> you tell me, and there's
> always e-mail —
> but what comfort can these be
> in a manhattan winter?
>
> *An Xiao*
> *New York, United States*

> Too tired to work,
> I lie down and dream
> about tropical islands
> where her brown form
> comes swaying to me.
>
> *M. Kei*
> *Chesapeake Bay, United States*

WINTER

the Seventies were
difficult times to get through,
the children were teens . . .
we, on different paths,
love took work in those days

Abigail Greene
United States

the voice of my kid
wakes me
rolling over
I feel
the morning of my wife

Sanford Goldstein
Japan

If I wasn't her father
I'd be just another bald man
watching dandelions
shed themselves
upon the wind.

Andrew Riutta
United States

that uncle —
how was I to know
as a ten-year child
his hand pressing my thighs
fingers touching my breast

Patricia Prime
New Zealand

my handsome son,
posed so that
his scarred arm
doesn't show
in the family photograph

M. Kei
Chesapeake Bay, United States

hugging
a load of knits
warm from the dryer
remembering a baby
now grown

susan delphine delaney
United States

WINTER

walking past
the Children's Hospital
reflecting
how proudly I love
my doctor daughter

Amelia Fielden
Australia

Like moth wings,
these ashes so soft.
Our cigarette dies,
and before we know it
we've shared a lifetime.

Andrew Riutta
United States

we wake in the dawn,
old friends and lovers still,
in our bed I feel
young again as you kiss
away my wrinkles

Abigail Greene
United States

FIRE PEARLS

With us from the start
twenty-one years ago
this stainless steel teapot
still reflects faces
now scratched and blurred

George Swede
Canada

how we have aged
you and I like spindrift
along the shore
until we are carried off
by tides of a greater sea

Marjorie A. Buettner
United States

purple swamp hen
uses the footbridge to cross
unlike i who have
no way to help you make
the transition to old age

Janice Bostok
Australia

WINTER

i brought home
my first born
with great trepidation
i enter his home to spend
my autumn days

Kala Ramesh
India

love and passion
in those early early years
came in brief spurts . . .
now at end-of-the-road eighty
find myself askew

Sanford Goldstein
Japan

one question
I never want answered:
should your memory
suddenly vanish
would you choose me again?

Janet Lynn Davis
Houston, Texas, United States

FIFTH SEASON

packing new luggage
for a long cruise at sea
a few things go in
solely for the attention
of unsuitable women

Michael McClintock
United States

home from a cruise
with another marriage proposal
Auntie laughs
Just imagine me
washing his socks

Marianne Bluger
Canada

trying to look her in
the eye as she explains
the Egyptian mummy—
her nipple-ring outlined beneath
the museum t-shirt

Larry Kimmel
United States

looking up
from the mini-manifesto
on her t-shirt,
I get this loathing look—"hey!
I'm a slow reader, okay?"

Larry Kimmel
United States

FIFTH SEASON

you enter my dreams
like a beggar
in the night . . .
i will not surrender
my womanly alms

Pamela A. Babusci
Rochester, New York, United States

my knight,
your perfection's gleam
enticed me;
now I thank you often . . .
for charming someone else

Janet Lynn Davis
Houston, Texas, United States

after our smiles
all in a flash;
I'm too old, she's too young
and furthermore
I'm married

Tom Clausen
United States

FIRE PEARLS

>You boast in print
>you've had a thousand women
>what's true?
>R.B. a thousand women
>had you

Marianne Bluger
Canada

>the handle
>of this racket,
>these green
>balls,
>and this celibate me!

Sanford Goldstein
Japan

>I miss him,
>my American man,
>his skin much darker than mine,
>tall, too, and well-hung,
>and oh, that Spanish baritone!

M. Kei
Chesapeake Bay, United States

FIFTH SEASON

the long slow crawl
of envy — eyes, shoulders, chests,
and below-waist visions:
endless nights of perpendiculars
rubbed in silence to standstill

Sanford Goldstein
Japan

I suppose
I shouldn't be so picky —
what else
should a trans girl expect but
lonely flings and a life of stares?

An Xiao
New York, United States

on leave
I follow a black girl
to the room
one touch is all
and my money's spent

Dave Bacharach
United States

FIRE PEARLS

> A full moon
> and coyotes howling—
> we're naked
> on our hands and knees
> in the prairie motel
>
> *George Swede*
> *Canada*

> I leave her place
> and see a man waiting
> where I once waited
> for some other man
> to leave her place
>
> *Dave Bacharach*
> *United States*

> let's not
> fall for each other
> this new guy tells me
> little metal cell phone
> hot on my ear
>
> *Laura Maffei*
> *United States*

FIFTH SEASON

Buddha,
Charles Bukowski and Bach . . .
taking my place
among the men in her life
that have come and gone

Andrew Riutta
United States

All I can give you
Is my body, my heart and
My undying soul.
Such inconsequential things.
They would not interest you.

Claire Elliott
United Kingdom

Our love cannot be.
I am not my own — I'll leave
and who'll protect you?
Amongst the ravens, pity
the poor bird that's beautiful.

Denis M. Garrison
United States

and still
there may be encounters
in this penny world,
and still the electric surge
of a look, a stare, a nod

Sanford Goldstein
Japan

"Tanglewood"
splintered and shotgunned
welcome sign—
your smouldering eyes,
scarlet lips and fingertips

Denis M. Garrison
United States

Beware, they say,
warning me against you
for you are incendiary
and I have been
too long from the flame

Angela Leuck
Canada

FIFTH SEASON

the timbre
of that voice strums
inner chords
I move toward her like a bead
along a slender chain

Kirsty Karkow
United States

peach slices
in thick cream
luscious
slick lips tell me
what I want to hear

Denis M. Garrison
United States

Haitian woman,
spawn of powerful genes—
work your spell
use your voodoo fingers
to enliven this old man

John Daleiden
United States

explore with me
possibility
between two mirrors . . .
your arched back
filtering stars

Robert D. Wilson
United States/Philippines

in the motel room
where three red flowers light up
the narrow stand,
twice he sheds his new nightshirt,
sometimes she hears a cat's wail

Sanford Goldstein
Japan

what we had
has surely vanished with the night
yet I awaken
cradled against your chest
my head upon your pillow

Thelma Mariano
Canada

FIFTH SEASON

Life is eternal
But love is so fickle and
Openly fleeting.
Why must my heart cling to the
Things that I can never keep?

Claire Elliott
United Kingdom

After we make love,
I spend the night staring
at the mountain of his shoulder
and the darkness of his skin,
hating his wife.

M. Kei
Chesapeake Bay, United States

no fear
of pregnancy she said
too good
to be true I thought
and I was right

Dave Bacharach
United States

FIRE PEARLS

In retrospect,
it would have been wiser
if we had skipped the sex
and gone straight
to the tearful breakup.

M. Kei
Chesapeake Bay, United States

how can i tame
his vagabond heart?
i am just a discarded love
on his endless trail
of broken promises

Pamela A. Babusci
Rochester, New York, United States

the black negligee
that I bought for your return
hangs in my closet
    day by day plums ripen
    and are picked clean by birds

Margaret Chula
United States

FIFTH SEASON

after the break-up
writing his name
in the dust . . .
outside my neighbor
dismembers a clinging vine

Pamela A. Babusci
Rochester, New York, United States

Tall reeds bending
in the strong east wind
and here I am
still thinking your words
cannot move me

Angela Leuck
Canada

the poets tell us
love is painful —
do you think
if I love you, you'll suffer
so very much?

Michael McClintock
United States

135

FIRE PEARLS

           Jan's ex
        is asking her
   to marry him again . . .
The streams have taken her head wreath
          too far . . .

Zhanna P. Rader
United States/Russia

His heart
is a skeleton key
that unlocks doors
that should never
be opened.

M. Kei
Chesapeake Bay, United States

With the same hope
that allows her to think of
this lone pear tree
as an orchard
she says, "I love you."

Andrew Riutta
United States

FIFTH SEASON

holding hands
we sit on the doorstep
of our first home
you assure me the ring
looks more expensive in the dark

Patricia Prime
New Zealand

afterwards
I offer him
the most unbroken
onion ring
in the bag

Laura Maffei
United States

my lips always tingled
when I kissed her—
true love, she whispered
I didn't say
cat allergy

Michael Dylan Welch
Sammamish, Washington, United States

she believed
he owned a string
of theatres
and married him, an usher
who liked to sleep late

Dave Bacharach
United States

long dark hair
tossed until it's tangled;
I use it
to sweep up the crumbs of me
you've failed to notice

Janet Lynn Davis
Houston, Texas, United States

explaining again
I swim through sentiments
of gratitude
deep love, frustration—
this familiar ocean

Amelia Fielden
Australia

FIFTH SEASON

caterpillars
eat enormous amounts
but for the emerging moths
and i when confronting you
there is no useful mouth

Janice Bostok
Australia

tightropes
passed over in those days
of the master's words,
the anguish of my wife
thrusting out fists of defiance

Sanford Goldstein
Japan

I bite
deep into her flesh
into her bone
the fantasy vanishes
and she's safe again

Dave Bacharach
United States

remembering you
pushing the dark warmth inside
outside a fearful roar
rolls the branches of trees
towards an electric flash

Janice Bostok
Australia

After you shadowed
my right eye
and I rouged
your left cheek
we ran out of make-up

George Swede
Canada

I am held
in this bed in this life
by your hands —
where would I be now
if I had said 'no'

Amelia Fielden
Australia

FIFTH SEASON

no bed
just one low pallet
and a quilt
in three minutes
it's over

Dave Bacharach
United States

rape (is) a nasty word,
it's taken years to spell it
out for all the world to see
do you still see me the same,
now that you know?

Abigail Greene
United States

to confess
the multiple taunts and stains
of those early years,
I refuse to take time to make a list,
I cannot simply chalk it off as youth

Sanford Goldstein
Japan

high tides threaten
to overwhelm the dock;
my daughter tells me
about the man
who hits her

M. Kei
Chesapeake Bay, United States

the third bitter year,
living in the same house and
waking up next to
the same man for a lifetime;
Lord, I've got to get out now!

Orestes
United States

all the years
Mother would turn her face
away
when Dad came home from work
each night and kissed her

Marianne Bluger
Canada

FIFTH SEASON

backdoors slammed
and often narrow beds
were caves of refuge—
we escaped loud kitchen noises,
red shirt stains, smells from tight lips

Sanford Goldstein
Japan

slow mantis
she will wait for you
she has time
after making supper
to sharpen knives

Denis M. Garrison
United States

this night
more than others
I'm tempted
to scratch my back
on that rusty nail

Andrew Riutta
United States

shall I find myself
in the love of this man
or in leaving him
or in nothing but these poems
written on airline napkins?

Laura Maffei
United States

"I know
that for a fact,"
she says, "the more you do
for men, the less respect they have
for you."

Zhanna P. Rader
United States/Russia

incoming tide —
shadows of trees undulate
reminding how
your rigid nature
appears to bend

Janice Bostok
Australia

FIFTH SEASON

Marital trauma
I write
another poem
about myself
as a frog

George Swede
Canada

What can you teach me,
old couple, that I have not
yet discovered? —
the sound of your
bickering as I sit alone

An Xiao
New York, United States

my shadow
worn thin through
neglect
for some time love's light
has not shone this way

André Surridge
New Zealand

FIRE PEARLS

so late
the nights you came back
without it
I finally understand
your heart

Brenda Humphrey-McMahen
Florida, United States

dealer man
turned my daughter on
to cocaine at age 15
he did his time
my daughter still doing coke

shanna baldwin moore
United States

You ask me about
My dating life, and I try
To hold back tears —
It's rarely a simple thing
For transgirls like me

An Xiao
New York, United States

FIFTH SEASON

moving out at last
I find her bottles stashed
in a secret place
I bury this as well
I cannot mourn for lies

Denis M. Garrison
United States

streetlights
illume the maples
from within . . .
was it so much, my love,
to expect the truth?

Larry Kimmel
United States

the black monkey man
has made him older
he slouches
with the weight of the darkness
that sucks him out of his own skin

shanna baldwin moore
United States

FIRE PEARLS

    A rough wind
    blows the waves
    against the current
    all those times
    I loved the wrong man

    Angela Leuck
    Canada

    moving house—
    there, under my desk,
    your lost photo
    smiling in sweet ignorance
    of cruel days ahead

    Denis M. Garrison
    United States

    if I ever find
    the world's most sour lemon,
    I'll give it to my ex and
    pucker his mouth
    shut forever

    M. Kei
    Chesapeake Bay, United States

FIFTH SEASON

burning ban:
love letters at the landfill
bear our names . . .
as if it might matter
to a million maggots

an'ya
United States

as I turn her brooch
to read the inscription
the pin draws blood
if she knew she still can hurt me
she would smile

Denis M. Garrison
United States

is it memory
that makes the long ago
more intense?
or is memory tricking me
into feeling I had the power?

Sanford Goldstein
Japan

FIRE PEARLS

no longer sharp
this pain of parting from you
I probe my heart
to find what else of value
may also now be missing

Beverley George
Pearl Beach. Australia

single again
she reads alone at night
the book of her heart
now closed
until further notice

Janet Lynn Davis
Houston, Texas, United States

since you left
I sleep very deeply
alone in our bed —
good practice, perhaps;
since coffins sleep only one

Denis M. Garrison
United States

APPENDIX A: RECOMMENDED READING

Beichman, Janine. *Embracing the Firebird.* Hawaii: University of Hawaii Press, 2002.
Better, Cathy Drinkwater, ed. *To Find the Moon.* Eldersburg, VA: Black Cat Press, 2004.
Emrich, Jeanne & Cathy Drinkwater Better, eds. *Something Like a Sigh.* Eldersburg, VA: Black Cat Press, 2005.
Hirshfield, Jane, trans. & ed. *The Ink Dark Moon.* New York: Vintage Books, 1990.
Lowitz, Leza, et al, trans. & eds. *A Long Rainy Season.* Berkeley, CA: Stone Bridge Press, 1994.
McClintock, Michael, et al, eds. *The Tanka Anthology.* Winchester, VA: Red Moon Press, 2003.
Reichhold, Jane & Werner Reichhold, eds. *Wind Five Folded.* Gualala, CA: AHA Books, 1994.
Saigyo. *Saigyo: Poems of a Mountain Home.* Trans. Burton Watson. New York: Columbia Univ. Press, 1991.
Shiki, Masaoka. *Songs from a Bamboo Village.* Trans. Sanford Goldstein & Seishi Shinoda. Vermont: Charles E. Tuttle, 1998.
Tasker, Brian, ed. *In the Ship's Wake.* North Shields, UK: Iron Press, 2001.
Tawara, Machi. *Salad Anniversary.* Trans. Juliet Winters Carpenter. Tokyo: Kodansha International, 1989.
Ueda, Makoto, trans & ed. *Modern Japanese Tanka.* New York: Columbia Univ. Press, 1996.
Ward, Linda Jeannette, ed. *Full Moon Tide.* Coinjock, NC: Clinging Vine Press, 2000.
Welch, Michael Dylan, ed. *Footsteps in the Fog.* Foster City, CA: Press Here, 1994.
—*Castles in the Sand.* Ibid., 2002.
Yosano, Akiko. *Tangled Hair.* Trans. Sanford Goldstein & Seishi Shinoda. Tokyo: Charles E. Tuttle, 1990.
Young, Karina, ed. *Searching for Echoes.* Salinas, CA: Tanka Society of America, 2003.

APPENDIX B: RESOURCE LIST

Organizations

Anglo-British Tanka Society:
   www.geocities.jp/nichieitanka/index.html
Japan Tanka Poets' Society: www.kajin.org/english.html
Tanka Canada: people.uleth.ca/~uzawa/TankaCanada.htm
Tanka Society of America: www.tankasocietyofamerica.com/

Online Resources

Tanka Central: TankaCentral.com
Kyoka Mad Poems (e-list): groups.google.com/group/kyoka
Tanka (e-list):: groups.yahoo.com/group/Tanka/
Tanka Fields (e-list)::
   groups.google.com/group/Tanka-Fields
CinquainPoets (e-list): tinyurl.com/hukh7

Journals - Print and Online

AHA Books: www.ahapoetry.com/ahalynx/212hmpg.html
American Tanka: AmericanTanka.com
Eucalypt: www.eucalypt.info
Gusts - see Tanka Canada
Kokako, New Zealand
Lynx: see AHA Books
Modern English Tanka: ModernEnglishTanka.com
Red Lights, USA
Ribbons - see Tanka Society of America
Simply Haiku: SimplyHaiku.com
Tanka Journal - see Japan Tanka Poets' Society
Tanka Splendor Award - see AHA Books

APPENDIX C: ACKNOWLEDGMENTS

Abbreviations used:
AT: American Tanka
AJTS: Anglo-Japanese Tanka Society website
BR: Bottle Rockets
BS: Blithe Spirit
FF: Footsteps in the Fog, Press Here, 1994
FLD: Five Lines Down
GS: Gusts, Tanka Canada
HH: Haiku Harvest
LX: Lynx
MET: Modern English Tanka
MR: Mirrors
NDR: Nisqually Delta Review
RB: Ribbons, Tanka Society of America
RL: Red Lights
RN: Raw NerVZ Haiku
SH: Simply Haiku
SW: In the Ship's Wake, Iron Press, 2001
TA: The Tanka Anthology, Red Moon, 2003
TC: Tanka Calendar, Winfred Press
TH: Tangled Hair
TJ: The Tanka Journal
TS: Tanka Splendor, AHA Books
WFF: Wind Five Folded, AHA Books
WHR: World Haiku Review
WN: Woodnotes
YM: Yellow Moon

an'ya. 'before you my life', 'burning ban', 'full of spring bulbs', 'must I too' & 'sidewalk café' *Moonstruck* 2006.

Babusci, Pamela A. 'fragments of lotus' *RL* Vol. 2. 2006; 'water lilies' *YM* Sum 2002; 'what words would' *AT* Spr 1997; 'when i think i know' *LX* XII:1 1997.

Bacharach, Dave. 'before snow fell' *MET* Fall 2006; 'I leave her place' & 'she asks' *SH* Fall 2005; 'my friend died' & 'she believed' *SH* Spr 2006; 'taking a walk' *SH* Sum 2006; 'this winter' *RB* Sum 2005; 'when I left' *RB* Sum 2006.

Barlow, John. 'before you move out', 'coming to bed', 'dawn', 'a half-moon', 'june', the sea', 'snow', 'the way you are sleeping' & 'your body' *Snow About To Fall* 2006.

Bluger, Marianne. 'home from a cruise' & 'all the years' *Nude with Scar,* 2006; 'You boast in print', 'With melting flakes', 'Spot my old flame' & 'Cold fire' *Zen Mercies, Small Satoris,* 2005.

Bostok, Janice. 'caterpillars', 'at dawn potted plants', 'embarrassed', 'Freya's heart shape', 'my hand reaches', 'purple swamp hen' & 'the sky' *Songs Once Sung* 2003; 'remembering you' *TS* 1997; 'the storm over' *YM* Win/Aut 1998.

Buettner, Marjorie A. 'the circling moon' *SH* Oct 2003; 'cool autumn's wind' *SW* 2001; 'a dark wind' & 'deep wilderness' *Woodpecker,* 6:1 2000; 'how we have aged' *TS* 2001; 'they say the moon' *TC* 2006.

Chula, Margaret. 'after many years', 'the black negligee' & 'saying good-bye' *Always Filling, Always Full* 2001; 'the stranger' *TC* 2005.

Clausen, Tom. 'after our smiles' *FLD* Sum 1994; 'after a rough day' *A Work of Love* 1997; 'after supporting' *LX* 12:1 1997; 'in the company of friends' *LX* 9:1 1994; 'a few leaves left' *LX* 2003; 'high clouds' *TC* 2006; 'my wife has learned' *Hermitage.* 2:1-2 2005; 'Queen Anne's Lace' *MR* Feb 1995; 'she's died so early' *LX* 2001; 'she's not here' *MR* Feb 1995.

Davis, Janet Lynn. 'her newborn face' *SH* Fall 2006; 'long dark hair' *Megaera* Sep 2006; 'each year', 'my knight' & 'my stolen' *MET* Fall 2006; 'single again' *RL* Jan 2006.

Delaney, Susan Delphine. 'hugging' *LX* Jun 1997.

Fielden, Amelia. 'Malay restaurant' & 'walking past' *Fountains Play* 2002.

Gadd, Benard. 'creek a vivid' & 'wind's bitter' *AJTS* Mar 2006.

Garrison, Denis M. 'knees dusted with snow' *LX* Jun 2006; 'moving house', 'since you left' *NDR* Win/Spr 2006; 'Our love cannot be' *Moonset* Spr 2006.

George, Beverley. 'no longer sharp' *RB* Spr 2006; 'rip-tide' *Int'l Tanka Contest.* 2005; 'salt on my tongue' *GS* #3, 2006.

Goldstein, Sanford. 'the handle' & 'the gorgeous' *This Tanka Whirl* 2001; 'backdoors slammed', 'the long slow crawl' & 'in the motel room' *Encounters in This Penny World* 2005; 'to love', 'my three tanka', 'rest', 'Tamura out into the sea' & 'the voice of my kid' *This Tanka World* 1977.

Harter, Penny. 'nun of your' *Lovepoems* 1981.

Humphrey-McMahen, Brenda. 'I sign' *AT #14,* 2004; 'from the window' *AT* #12 2002; 'at his request' *LX* Feb 2004.

Karkow, Kirsty. 'frozen pond' *YM* Sum 2003; 'deep in snow' *Kokako* Sum 2003.

Kei, M. 'Awake in bed I' *MyTown* Jul 2006; 'The comb she dropped' *HH* Sum 2006; 'When my boys are here' & 'I was not lonely' *SH* Sum 2006; 'that man' *MET* Fall 2006.

Kimmel, Larry. 'along the river' *WN* Spr 1996; 'the dawn's gray effusion' *LX* Jun 2002; 'a drizzly day' *AT* Fall 1998; 'Fist poised to knock' *LX* May/Jun 1999; 'her breast fits' *Green Age Literary Review* Spr 1985; 'her laughter' *Hummingbird* Mar 1998; 'her skirt brightens' *Lights Across the River* 1997; 'I couldn't help myself' *BR* #12 2005; 'looking up' *LX* Jan, 2001; 'in the night-fog' *TS* 2000; 'our old table' & 'streetlights' *AT* Fall 1999; 'stark from the shower' *LX* Feb 1996; 'this moonless night' *RN* Fall 1996; 'this time, she tells me' *TJ* #26 2005; 'the tilt' *still* #4 2000; 'trying to look' *RL* Jan 2005.

Leuck, Angela. 'Beware, they say' *GS* Fall/Win 2005; 'Gazing out', 'Racing home' 'Sleepless tonight' & 'Tall reeds bending' *SH* Sum 2005; 'Going out to view' *Invisible Tea* 2006; 'Hanging out the wash' *AT* Spr 2002; 'A rough wind' *LX* Feb 2006; 'Sampling' *LX* Oct 2001; 'Snowy morning' *TS* 2005; 'This morning' *TS* 2004; 'You painted over' *Tanka in the Light* Sep 2001; 'The time' *BR* #13 2005.

Maffei, Laura. 'afterwards', 'let's not', 'shall I find myself' & 'so handsome' *drops from her umbrella* 2006.

Mariano, Thelma. 'on the beach that night' *Castles in the Sand* 2002; 'in the breeze' *AT* Spr 2003; 'the fluid motion' *LX* Oct 2004; 'late in the season' *TS* 2004; 'maybe we'll meet again' *AT* Spr 2004; 'moonlight filters' *GS* Spr/Sum 2005; 'years on my own' *TA*.

McClintock, Michael. 'biting' *Man With No Face* 1974; 'between sun and shade' & 'no net' *Letters in Time* 2005; 'foolish' & 'you never showed up' *BS* Dec 2003; 'from my hill' *Moonset* #3, 2006; 'next door' *AT* #9, 2000; 'the poets tell us' *TA*; 'traveling a country' *MET* Fall 2006; 'well-loved and wise' *RB* Jun 2005; 'when you opened' *TS* 2004.

Ness, Pamela Miller. 'Beneath' *Castles in the Sand*. 2002; 'deep' *Hummingbird.* Sep 2001; 'Like Gauguin's' *RN* X:1 2005; 'Sultry dawn' *TJ* Spr 2003; 'Sultry night' *only the bulbs* 2004.

Ramesh, Kala. 'my worn out sandals' & 'seeing m children' *Loch Raven Review* Fall 2005; 'the thrill' *SH* Sum 2006; 'truth lies' *MET* FAll 2006; 'our heads so close' *WHR* 5:2 2005; 'when alive I wanted' *SH* Win 2005.

Riutta, Andrew. 'every road' *SH* Fall 2005; 'this night' *MET* Fall 2006.

Robinson, Chad Lee. 'for the scent' *RB* Win 2005; 'tired of arguing' *RL* Jan 2005.

Simser, Guy. 'Nose so pressed' *still* #2 2001.

Singh, R. K. 'One thousand miles' *LX* Oct 2004; 'She is no moon' *LX* Feb 2005; 'She senses all things' *LX* Feb 2005.

Smarandescu, Vasile. 'I harness the horse' & 'water in the well' *The Evening Passenger* 2001.

Swede, George. 'After you shadowed' *As Far As The Sea Can Eye* 1979; 'Another day closer' *The Plaza* 1990; 'In the living room' *GS* Spr/Sum 2006; 'the piano idle for weeks' *RB* Win 2005; 'With us from the start' *My Shadow Doing Something* 1997.

Ward, Linda Jeannette. 'I cannot scatter' *TS* 1999; 'pressed' *BS* Dec 2005; 'a volley of hailstones' *BS* Sep 2003;

Welch, Michael Dylan. 'morning sun' *FF* 1994; 'I am awake tonight' *Fresh Hot Bread* Feb 2002; 'my lips always tingled' *LX* Jun 1997; 'the salt and pepper' *LX* Jun 1998; 'so lonely' *WN* Aut 1993; 'you speak of the distance' *LX* Jun 1998.

Xiao, An. 'I suppose' & 'dreaming of lola' *SH* Spr 2006.

INDEX OF POETS

an'ya 12, 18, 49, 55, 89, 149
Babusci, Pamela A. 51, 61, 82, 115, 125, 134, 135
Bacharach, Dave 20, 24, 61, 72, 81, 86, 89, 92, 107, 127, 128, 133, 138, 139, 141
Barlow, John 22, 25, 39, 84, 86, 97, 98, 100, 102
Bluger, Marianne 36, 73, 74, 124, 126, 142
Bostok, Janice 18, 21, 28, 29, 34, 52, 78, 105, 110, 111, 113, 120, 139, 140, 145
Buettner, Marjorie A. 16, 40, 68, 69, 80, 98, 120
Chula, Margaret 31, 37, 41, 47, 50, 54, 63, 71, 100, 134
Clausen, Tom 29, 33, 45, 52, 65, 77, 92, 104, 106, 109, 125
Dale, Magdalena 56
Daleiden, John 20, 21, 24, 46, 47, 48, 67, 106, 112, 131
Davis, Janet Lynn 25, 35, 75, 121, 125, 138, 150
delaney, susan delphine 62, 87, 90, 101, 104, 118
Elliott, Claire 71, 129, 133
Fielden, Amelia 103, 119, 138, 140
Gadd, Bernard 22, 25, 41, 42, 83
Garrison, Denis M. 44, 62, 73, 91, 111, 129, 130, 131, 143, 147, 148, 149, 150
George, Beverley 41, 42, 54, 150
Goldstein, Sanford 12, 32, 48, 50, 75, 93, 104, 107, 113, 114, 117, 121, 126, 127, 130, 132, 139, 141, 149

Goode, Michael R. 99
Greene, Abigail 16, 27, 31, 45, 74, 78, 79, 100, 117, 119, 141
Harter, Penny 33, 80, 81, 92
Humphrey-McMahen, Brenda 33, 34, 49, 62, 65, 82, 85, 87, 110, 146
Kacian, Jim 35, 69, 83
Karkow, Kirsty 106, 114, 131
Kei, M. 28, 34, 37, 56, 58, 60, 64, 69, 72, 85, 95, 101, 107, 108, 115, 116, 118, 126, 133, 134, 136, 142, 148
Kimmel, Larry 14, 19, 23, 30, 32, 36, 43, 58, 60, 64, 84, 91, 96, 97, 124, 147
Leuck, Angela 12, 15, 20, 40, 45, 47, 53, 60, 87, 90, 96, 102, 130, 135, 148
Lindsey, Darrell 26
Lockhart, J. Andrew 14, 24, 30, 88
Maffei, Laura 77, 105, 128, 137, 144
Mariano, Thelma 18, 30, 52, 58, 70, 83, 85, 86, 102, 114, 132
McClintock, Michael 11, 15, 17, 43, 53, 57, 59, 81, 84, 91, 93, 97, 112, 123, 135
moore, shanna baldwin 76, 146, 147
Neal, Dustin 14, 22, 53, 56, 63, 64, 74, 96, 108, 115
Neily, Larry 108
Ness, Pamela Miller 17, 46, 99
Orestes 19, 42, 44, 55, 70, 71, 142
Papanicolaou, Linda Morey 76
Prewitt, Jack 19, 88
Prime, Patricia 17, 21, 68, 75, 90, 103, 113, 118, 137

Rader, Zhanna 51, 59, 80, 93, 136, 144
Ramesh, Kala 37, 40, 61, 76, 99, 110, 112, 121
Riutta, Andrew 44, 67, 117, 119, 128, 136, 143
Robinson, Chad Lee 13, 48, 50
Simser, Guy 98
Singh, R. K. 26, 82, 111
Smarandescu, Vasile 13, 73
Surridge, André 13, 16, 26, 89, 101, 116, 145
Swede, George 28, 29, 49, 51, 72, 79, 120, 128, 140, 145
Ward, Linda Jeannette 35, 57, 109
Welch, Michael Dylan 23, 27, 36, 78, 103, 105, 137
Wilson, Robert 32, 43, 46, 54, 55, 59, 88, 132
Xiao, An 15, 23, 27, 31, 57, 63, 109, 116, 127, 145, 146